This book belongs to: